THE BIRTH OF JESUS

and other Bible stories

p^3

The city of Sodom

GENESIS 18–19

One day, God spoke to Abraham and told him that he was concerned about the people who lived in the cities of Sodom and Gomorrah. "These people don't respect me at all," he said. "Instead they do as much evil as they like. I will destroy them and their cities."

Abraham knew that his nephew, Lot, and his family lived in Sodom and was horrified at the thought of them dying. He asked, "Lord, are you really going to destroy the good people along with the guilty? I know you are a fair and just judge. What if there are fifty good people living there? Would you punish them, too?"

God replied, "No, if I find fifty good people living in Sodom I will allow the city to remain standing."

Abraham trembled before God, wanting to ask him to be even more merciful. "Forgive my boldness, and do not be angry with me, but what if there are only twenty good people, or even only ten?"

God replied, "If there are just ten good people, I will not destroy the city."

That evening, two angels, who looked like ordinary men, went to Sodom and met Abraham's nephew, Lot, at the city gate.

Lot bowed before them, and said, "Gentlemen, I am here to serve you. Please come to my house and stay the night." So they went, and Lot prepared a meal for them.

Later, a large crowd of rowdy men from the city gathered outside the house and demanded that Lot hand over the two strangers so that they could ill-treat them.

Lot pleaded desperately with them not to do such a terrible thing, saying, "I must protect my guests, at all costs. You can even take my daughters instead!"

But the crowd only grew wilder and prepared to force their way into Lot's house. Then the two angels came to Lot's rescue. They pulled him back into the house and blinded the men outside, so that they could not find the door and break in.

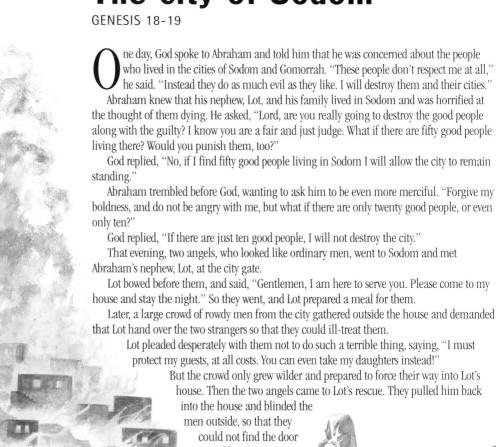

THE CITIES OF SODOM AND GOMORRAH

Sodom and Gomorrah were probably once located at the south-east end of the Dead Sea. The remains of the two cities may now lie under its waters. Archaeological evidence shows that this was once a fertile, well-watered area with a large population.

Lot and his wife

GENESIS 19

The two angels now gave Lot a serious warning. "If you have any family living in Sodom, you must hurry and get them out of here," the angels urged him. "God has sent us to destroy this city and every wicked person who lives in it!"

As dawn broke the next morning, the angels again urged Lot to leave. But he still was not sure what to do. It was hard to believe that God was about to destroy his home. Seeing his hesitation, the angels grabbed Lot, his wife and his two daughters by the hands and led them out of the city.

"Quickly!" the angels shouted. "Time is running out. Run into the hills and save your lives! And there is one thing you must remember – do not look back!"

Lot and his family hurried away, and as the sun rose high in the sky, God sent a devastating storm of burning sulfur raining down on the cities of Sodom and Gomorrah. Nothing survived the inferno. Everyone died and all the buildings and land lay in ruins.

Sensing the destruction behind her, Lot's wife could not resist turning round and looking back at the city, disobeying the angels' warning. Immediately, she was transformed into a solid pillar of salt.

Early the next morning, Abraham looked down at Sodom and Gomorrah. All he could see were puffs of smoke rising up from where the cities had once stood. At least his nephew Lot had escaped to safety, he thought with relief.

SALTY DEAD SEA
At 1,285 feet below sea-level, the Dead Sea is the lowest point on earth. It has no outlet, so it loses water only through evaporation. This leaves such a high concentration of minerals and salts in the water that nothing can live there. The pillars of salt in the water are reminders of the fate of Lot's wife.

God calls Isaiah to be a prophet

ISAIAH 6

God chose Isaiah to be one of his greatest prophets, to warn and encourage the nation of Judah to return to obeying his ways. One day, he gave Isaiah an amazing vision.

"In the year that King Uzziah died, I saw God sitting on his throne in all his might and majesty," Isaiah explained with wonder. "Angels flew above him, covering their faces and feet with their wings, and shaking the building with their powerful voices as they called out, 'Holy, holy, holy are you, Lord God Almighty! Your glory fills the whole earth.'

"I felt overwhelmed at the utter holiness of my God, the one who is perfect and pure. So I cried out, 'I am a sinner, Lord, not clean enough to stand in your presence!' An angel flew over to me with a glowing, hot coal in his hand, taken from the holy altar. As he touched my lips with it, he said, to my relief, 'Now your guilt is taken away and your sins are forgiven.'

"Then God himself asked, 'Who is willing to be my messenger?'

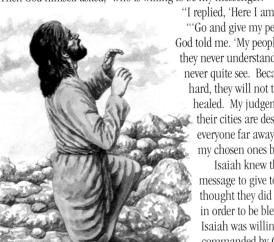

"I replied, 'Here I am, Lord. Send me!'

"'Go and give my people this message,' God told me. 'My people always listen, but they never understand. They look, but they never quite see. Because their hearts are hard, they will not turn to me and be healed. My judgement will last until their cities are destroyed and I send everyone far away, leaving only a few of my chosen ones behind.'"

Isaiah knew that this was a severe message to give to God's people, who thought they did not need to obey God in order to be blessed by him. But Isaiah was willing to do as he was commanded by God.

Hezekiah cries for healing

ISAIAH 38

A t the very time that King Hezekiah needed to be a strong leader to fight the Assyrians who were threatening to attack Jerusalem, he became gravely ill. A boil erupted on his skin and spread infection all over his body until he was almost dying.

The prophet Isaiah went to see him and told him, "God says you won't recover from this illness, so you must hurry and put your affairs in order before you die."

Hezekiah's heart sank with despair. With tears streaming down his face, he turned his face to the wall and prayed, "Lord God, please remember that I have loved you sincerely and always tried to do good. Must the best years of my life be cut short like this? Listen to my cries, O God, and help me!"

God gave Isaiah another message for the sick king.

"Tell Hezekiah that I have heard his tearful prayer and will give him another fifteen years to live. And by the strength of my hand, I will defend Jerusalem from her Assyrian attackers. Watch and see! As a sign that my promise will come true, I will make the shadow cast by the sundial move back ten paces."

Then Isaiah told the king to take a thick mixture of figs, and to apply it as medicine to the boil. Hezekiah did this and was healed completely, and he watched in awe as indeed the sundial's shadow moved back ten paces.

"I praise you, loving God, for saving me from death," Hezekiah joyfully wrote afterwards. "My suffering has made me humble and I will spend the rest of my days singing about your faithfulness."

ASSYRIAN STONE CARVING

The Assyrians established a line of fierce warrior-kings and conquered a great empire. They decorated their palaces with stone carvings of huge winged monsters, with the bodies of bulls or lions, and bearded human faces. Lion-hunting was the sport of the kings of Assyria and the animal was regarded as a royal beast. In the time of Isaiah, Judah was the only nation the Assyrians did not conquer, although it had to pay the Assyrians an annual tribute of goods and crops.

FANNING THE FIRE
This wooden model from Egypt shows a man fanning a charcoal fire, which was probably used for cooking. Food was normally boiled in a pot over an open fire. To bake bread, large, flat stones were heated in the fire. When the dough was ready, the hot stones were taken out of the fire and the dough was placed on them to cook.

SPICES
Like other ancient peoples, the Babylonians used spices to flavor their foods. One of the most commonly used spices was the herb cumin. It was grown for its aromatic seeds, which were ground up and used in place of pepper.

A DIET OF VEGETABLES
The diet of vegetables that Daniel requested would have been fairly limited. Many vegetables, such as cucumbers, were eaten raw. Others, such as lentils, beans and leeks, were boiled in water or oil. Seasoning with garlic or cumin helped to give some flavor to what was otherwise a rather boring diet.

Trained for the king's service
DANIEL 1

When the Babylonians captured Jerusalem, they selected a group of Israelites who had useful skills and took them back to Babylon. One of these men was called Daniel.

The Babylonian king, Nebuchadnezzar, ordered his chief official to select the very best of these young men. They were to be trained to help him rule his kingdom.

Daniel was willing to work hard for the king, but he also wanted to remain faithful to God.

When he realized that he would have to eat the same food and wine as the king, including foods forbidden by his faith, Daniel asked the chief official if he could eat a plainer diet.

"I am sorry, Daniel," the official said, sympathetically, "but the king has ordered you to eat his food. If you do not eat it and become weaker than the others, he will execute me!"

So instead, Daniel appealed to his guard. "Feed my three friends and me only vegetables and water for ten days. Then see whether we suffer or not."

The guard agreed. At the end of the ten days of their new diet, Daniel and his friends looked fitter and healthier than the Israelites who had eaten the royal food, so they were allowed to continue.

As Daniel followed his training, God gave him great knowledge and wisdom, and the gift of understanding dreams and visions. At the end of three years, the king questioned Daniel and found that he was much cleverer than his magicians. So Daniel became the king's servant.

Daniel explains the king's dream

DANIEL 2

King Nebuchadnezzar was tormented by a troubling nightmare that he could not understand, so he summoned all his wise men.

"You should be able to tell me exactly what was in my dream and what it means, without me giving you any details!" he insisted. "Unless you answer, I will have you all executed!"

"But only the gods can reveal such things," the wise men protested. At this, the furious king ordered that they should all be put to death, including Daniel and his friends.

Wisely, Daniel asked the king for more time. Then he went home and prayed that God would spare their lives by showing him what the dream meant. To Daniel's relief, God revealed the mystery to him in a vision.

"No man, including me, is clever enough to explain your dream," Daniel humbly told the king the next day, "but there is a God in heaven who can reveal all mysteries." Daniel explained that the dream foretold what would happen in the future.

"You saw an enormous and terrifying statue of a man," he told the king. "It had a gold head, a silver body, and bronze legs. As you were watching, a rock smashed the statue's feet which were made of iron mixed with clay.

"Then every part of the statue was smashed into tiny pieces that were blown away by the wind, leaving no trace. But the rock itself became a huge mountain which covered the whole world.

"Your Majesty, the gold represents your mighty kingdom, and the other parts of the statue represent other, less great kingdoms. And the rock that destroyed them all is God's eternal kingdom that, one day, will cover the whole world."

The king realized that Daniel was speaking the truth, and showed his appreciation by making him the ruler of the whole province of Babylon.

BABYLONIAN BOUNDARY STONE
The Babylonians kept records on clay tablets or stones. Sometimes records of who owned the land were made public and the stones would be set up in the field or temple to which the agreement related. Boundary stones like this one were marked with the symbols of the gods and goddesses who were believed to have witnessed the contract.

THE BABYLONIAN EMPIRE
The Babylonians reached the height of their power in about 600BC, during the reign of King Nebuchadnezzar. At this time, they controlled a huge empire, stretching from the Mediterranean Sea in the west to the Persian Gulf in the east. The story of Daniel takes place just after the Babylonians had conquered Jerusalem, in 586BC.

Signs of the zodiac
Astrologers believe that the stars and planets exert a decisive influence on a person's character and destiny. Astrology flourished in Babylon under the influence of the priests. The zodiac and its twelve signs are thought to have originated there. The Bible rejects beliefs such as astrology, because God alone has control over the universe which he created.

THE ANGEL GABRIEL

The angel Gabriel was sent to give Zechariah the news of John the Baptist's birth. Gabriel was God's special messenger, and his name means either "God is my hero" or "Mighty man of God". Gabriel and Michael are the only angels in the Bible to be mentioned by name.

INCENSE ALTAR

A gold incense altar stood before the Most Holy Place in the temple. A priest had to keep the incense burning on the altar and make sure there was a fresh supply before the morning sacrifice and after the evening sacrifice. This was a great honor and priests were chosen by lot. Zechariah was chosen in this way.

GALBANUM

One of the ingredients used in the sacred incense burnt on the altar was galbanum, an aromatic resin from a plant related to fennel which grew in Syria and Persia. The other ingredients for the sacred incense were gum resin, onycha (which came from mollusc shells) and frankincense.

Zechariah is promised a son

LUKE 1

Zechariah was a priest during the reign of King Herod. Both he and his wife, Elizabeth, were humble followers of God, obeying all his commands. They were now old and their lives were sad because they did not have any children.

One day, as part of his priestly duties, Zechariah was chosen to burn incense on the altar. As he was going about his task, an angel came and stood next to the altar. Zechariah was terrified, but the angel calmed him saying, "Don't be afraid. After all these years your prayers have been answered. Elizabeth will have a son called John. Not only will he give you much happiness, but his birth will bring great joy to many people. He will be filled with the Lord's Spirit from birth and will persuade many Israelites to return to God. Above all else, he is destined to prepare the way for the coming of the Lord himself."

"How can I know that what you are saying is true?" stammered Zechariah. "Surely Elizabeth and I are too old to have a child now?"

"I, Gabriel, have come from the very presence of the Lord to bring you this wonderful message. But because you have doubted me, you will be unable to speak until the day that the child is born," the angel answered before disappearing.

Outside, the crowds were wondering why Zechariah was taking so long. When he finally emerged, they knew that he had seen a vision because he was unable to talk to them.

Elizabeth became pregnant, just as the angel had said, and in due course she gave birth to the promised child. All her relatives were overjoyed for her sake.

When they took the baby to be circumcised they were ready to call him Zechariah, but Elizabeth intervened,

"No, we want to call him John."

Everyone was surprised because there was nobody in the family with such a name, so they asked Zechariah what the boy should be called. They handed him a writing slate and were amazed when in clear, bold letters he wrote the name "John". No sooner had he done so than he was able to speak once more and gave praise to the Lord.

Everybody who heard what had happened was intrigued and began to wonder about the special future that lay ahead of the boy.

Trusting what God says
Sometimes it seems impossible to believe what God says to us. Like Zechariah, we may be full of doubts that God's will for us can come true. By taking one step at a time, we can ask God how he's going to make our dreams happen, and then watch him provide what we need.

An angel brings news for Mary

LUKE 1

Six months into Elizabeth's pregnancy God sent Gabriel to Nazareth in Galilee where Mary lived. She was engaged to Joseph who could trace his family tree back to King David.

"Greetings, chosen one of God. God is with you," the angel said. Poor Mary was frightened by this introduction and trembled with fear.

"Don't be alarmed, Mary. God is pleased to bless you. You are going to have a child called Jesus. He will be called the Son of the Most High God. God will give him David's kingdom and establish him as king over the house of Jacob for ever."

"How is this possible?" Mary queried. "I am not yet married to Joseph."

Gabriel replied, "The power of the Holy Spirit will rest upon you. So the child that is to be born will be called the Son of God. Even your cousin Elizabeth is expecting a son in her old age. Nothing is beyond the power of God."

Mary was speechless. All she could say before the angel left was, "May everything that you have spoken to God's humble servant come true."

Mary soon packed her belongings and paid a visit to Elizabeth. When they met, the child in Elizabeth's womb leapt for joy, and speaking with the inspiration of the Holy Spirit, Elizabeth proclaimed, "You are blessed among all women and the child you are carrying is blessed too. To what do I owe this honor that the mother of my Lord has come to see me? When I heard you speak, my child danced inside my body. You will indeed be blessed because you have believed the words of the Lord!"

When Mary heard what Elizabeth said, she declared, "May my soul give glory to God, for he has looked upon his humble servant. From this day onwards everyone shall call me blessed because the all-powerful God has done something remarkable for me. He always shows mercy to those who honor him and he humbles the self-confident. He dethrones kings and exalts the humble. He satisfies the hungry and sends the rich away empty-handed. He has not forgotten his people Israel but has remembered the promise he made to our father Abraham."

Mary remained with Elizabeth for three months and then she went home to Nazareth.

GABRIEL BRINGS NEWS TO MARY
The angel Gabriel was active in the preparations for the birth of Jesus. First sent by God to Zechariah, he then went to Mary to announce to her that she would become the mother of the Messiah, God's promised Saviour. This is called the Annunciation, and is a popular subject in religious art. Although Christians often refer to Gabriel as an archangel, the term is not used in the Bible.

Nazareth
The village of Nazareth, which was the home of Mary and Joseph, lay in the Roman province of Galilee. It is 20 miles from the Mediterranean coast, 15 miles west of the Sea of Galilee and about 70 miles north of Jerusalem. Although close to a number of important trade routes, it was a small and isolated village. Archaeological remains suggest that ancient Nazareth was higher up the hill than the present village.

God reassures Joseph

MATTHEW 1

Then Joseph realized that Mary was expecting a baby before they were married, he was terribly upset. She had always seemed so pure and lovely, he never imagined she would be unfaithful to him with another man.

Sadly, Joseph knew that he could not marry her, but being kind, he decided to break their engagement quietly, so that she would not suffer too much public shame and disgrace.

Joseph was still thinking about his disappointment, when God's angel appeared to him in a dream with a reassuring message. "Don't be upset, Joseph," the angel said. "Go ahead and marry Mary, because it is God himself who has conceived the child by the power of the Holy Spirit. And when the boy is born, you are to name him Jesus, because he will save his people from their sins."

When Joseph woke up, he felt relieved that, after all, Mary had not sinned with another man. And he was proud and excited that as a descendant of the mighty King David, it would be through his family that the eagerly awaited Messiah would be born.

Being a righteous man who trusted God, Joseph obeyed and quickly married Mary as they had planned. But he did not sleep with her until after she gave birth to her son, Jesus.

JOSEPH
The Roman Catholic, Eastern Orthodox and Episcopal churches honor Joseph as a saint. We know little about his life after he and his family settled in Nazareth, but we are told that he was a craftsman or carpenter. Early Christian legends portrayed him as an aging widower with children of his own when he married Mary, but marriage customs of the day make it much more likely that he was in his mid-teens when they married.

Born in a stable

LUKE 2

ot long before Mary was due to give birth, the Roman emperor, Augustus, ordered everyone to register in their home towns so they could be counted in order to work out how much tax to collect. So Joseph loaded his donkey with a few possessions and took Mary on the long journey south from Nazareth to Bethlehem, which was the town of his ancestor, David.

When they arrived, Mary and Joseph were exhausted and looked forward to a good night's sleep in one of the town's inns. But Bethlehem was so full of visitors that there wasn't an empty room anywhere. Joseph was worried because it was nearly time for Mary to have her baby. Eventually, they found a stable and decided that they would rest there.

When Mary gave birth to her son, she wrapped him snugly in strips of cloth to keep him warm and secure, then laid him gently in a manger full of hay where the animals fed, so he could sleep comfortably.

Joseph and Mary were delighted with their new baby son and called him Jesus, just as the angel had told them to.

MADONNA AND CHILD
Over the centuries the virgin Mary, the Madonna, has been a popular subject for works of art. According to legend, Luke was the first to paint a picture of the Madonna, although the oldest known pictures of her are in the catacombs of the early Christians just outside Rome. The Madonna and child together have also been an important source of inspiration for artists.

COINS OF CAESAR AUGUSTUS
Caesar Augustus was the first, and perhaps the greatest, Roman emperor. Augustus means "exalted" – a title which the Roman Senate awarded him in 27BC. His rule (31BC–AD14) was a golden age in Roman literature and architecture.

THE CHURCH OF THE NATIVITY IN BETHLEHEM
Built in AD325, this is said to be the oldest Christian Church in existence. The low "Door of Humility" stopped people riding into the church. Today, Roman Catholic, Greek Orthodox and Armenian Christians share the church.

The shepherds and the wise men

MATTHEW 2; LUKE 2

I n the fields nearby, some shepherds were keeping an eye on their sheep. Suddenly an angel appeared to them and their eyes were dazzled by the glory of God.

The shepherds were overcome with fear, but the angel reassured them. "Do not be afraid. I come to you with a message of great happiness for everyone. This very night, in the quiet back streets of Bethlehem, the Saviour has been born. You will know that what I have told you is true when you discover the child, neatly wrapped in strips of cloth and lying in a manger."

As soon as the angel had finished speaking, the dark night sky was filled with a huge crowd of angels, all praising God. "Glory to God and peace to all the peoples of the earth," they sang.

When the angels disappeared, the shepherds raced off to Bethlehem and found Jesus, exactly as the angel had told them. After paying their respects to Joseph and Mary, they told everyone they met about the unique baby boy.

Soon, other visitors came looking for Jesus. Wise men from a distant eastern country arrived in Jerusalem and began making inquiries about the presence of a new king.

"For many days we have followed a star that will lead us to him. We want to worship the new king and present him with gifts," they said.

When King Herod learnt of their arrival, he was alarmed and quizzed his advisors about the possible birthplace of the long-awaited Saviour. They told him about one prophecy which predicted that the Saviour would be born in Bethlehem.

Then, unknown to anyone else, Herod spoke to the wise men and discovered how long they had been following the star. He directed them to Bethlehem saying, "When you discover the child, let me know, so that I can come and worship him as well."

So the wise men set off for Bethlehem, following the star until it came to a halt above where Jesus was staying. They entered the house, their hearts pounding with joy at the thought that their long journey was at an end.

When they saw Jesus, they fell on their knees and worshipped him. Then they opened their bags to reveal the precious presents that they had brought: gold, frankincense and myrrh.

When they left, the wise men did not go to see King Herod because they had been warned in a dream to return home without going back to Jerusalem.

THE WISE MEN'S JOURNEY
The Bible says that the wise men, or magi, had traveled from the east. They could have come from Persia, Babylonia, or southern Arabia. We do not know how many wise men there were, although it is often assumed that there were three of them, because they brought three gifts.

Great rejoicing!

LUKE 2

When Jesus was just a few weeks old, Mary and Joseph took him to the temple in Jerusalem to present him to God, as the law required. They offered two young birds as a sacrifice of thanks for the gift of a child.

There was a devout man in Jerusalem, called Simeon. God had promised him that he would not die before he had seen the Christ, the anointed one of God.

Led by the Holy Spirit, Simeon entered the temple while Jesus and his parents were there. Shaking with excitement, Simeon asked if he could hold the baby in his arms.

As he cradled Jesus close to his chest, Simeon praised God: "Lord of all, now I can die in peace, for you have kept your promise to me. With my own eyes I can see the child who will bring your salvation. He will bring glory to Israel and be a light to the Gentiles."

Mary and Joseph were astounded as they listened to his words. Then Simeon turned to them and whispered to Mary, "Your child will bring joy to many people. But he will also provoke anger in the hearts of many in this land and will cause you great pain, too."

Scarcely had Simeon finished speaking, than they were approached by another stranger. She was an elderly prophet, called Anna, who was continually in the temple fasting and praying.

When she saw Jesus, Anna too gave thanks to God. She talked endlessly about Jesus to everyone who was longing for the time when God would come and set Jerusalem free.

When Joseph and Mary had carried out their obligations, they returned to their home in Nazareth. As the years passed, Jesus grew into a child full of God's grace and wisdom.

OFFERING A SACRIFICE

Forty days after the birth of a child, the Jewish law required a mother to go to the temple to offer a sacrifice of thanksgiving. The normal sacrifice was a lamb and a pigeon, or dove, but poor people were allowed to present two pigeons or doves instead.

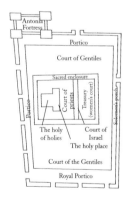

PRESENTATION IN THE TEMPLE

The law stipulated that the firstborn child was to be dedicated to serve in the temple. In a ceremony, parents paid money to the priests who served there in place of the firstborn son.

COURTS OF THE TEMPLE

This floor plan shows the layout of the temple courtyards in Herod's day. Anyone was permitted to enter the Court of the Gentiles, but only Jews were allowed to go into the Inner Court. Mary would have been able to enter the Treasury or Women's Court, while men could go into the Court of Israel.

Water jars
*Water vessels were sometimes
made from gold, silver or ivory.
But by far the most common and
practical way of carrying and
storing water was in large jars
made from stone or pottery. The
porous earthenware would
absorb some of the liquid, which
helped to stop it evaporating and
kept it cool. The largest jars could
hold over 27 gallons of water.*

*The Law required Jews to
cleanse themselves ritually,
especially before a meal or
religious ceremony, and so
several water jars would have
been needed at the wedding for
the ritual washing of hands and
utensils. The wine would have
been drawn from these jars and
served from jugs.*

Water becomes wine

JOHN 2

On one occasion Jesus, his mother Mary and his disciples were guests at a wedding in the Galilean town of Cana.

During the feast, the wine ran out, so Mary told her son, "The wine has run out; there is none left to drink."

Jesus replied, "Why are you telling me about this? It is not my responsibility. It is not the right time for me to act."

Nevertheless, Mary attracted the attention of some of the servants and, nodding in Jesus' direction, she whispered, "Do whatever that man tells you."

They approached Jesus and told him what his mother had said. Jesus looked at Mary (who was busy avoiding his glance) and said to them, "Fill those jars with water," and he pointed to six stone water jars, of the sort used in ritual washing and that had been lying in a secluded corner. They were very large – each one could hold about twenty five gallons.

The servants did as he told them and when they reported back to him he said, "Pour out a little and give it to the master of the banquet to taste."

So the servants took some to the master of the banquet and asked him to taste it. He had no idea where the drink had come from, but sipped some, letting it linger in his mouth before swallowing it.

It was delicious. Privately he congratulated the bridegroom. "Normally the best wine is served first so that by the time it has run out and only inferior wine is left, the guests have drunk too much to notice the difference. You, however, have kept the best wine until last!"

This was the first miracle that Jesus performed and in so doing he showed the first glimpse of his glory, and his disciples put their trust in him.

Jesus heals the lepers

MARK 1; LUKE 17

M any of the people who came to Jesus suffered from leprosy. One day a leper approached Jesus and fell on his knees in front of him, crying out in his desperation, "If you want to, you have the power to make me well again!"

Jesus felt sorry for the man and stretched out his hand and touched him gently. "Of course I want to," Jesus said. "Be healed!"

As he spoke, the man was cured of his leprosy.

Jesus sent the man on his way, but as he did so he told him, "You must not tell anyone what has happened to you. Instead go to the priests and make the offerings as instructed in the book of Moses."

But the man paid no attention to what Jesus had said. As soon as Jesus had gone, the man began to explain to everyone what Jesus had done for him.

Another time, as Jesus was traveling to Jerusalem, he was met by ten lepers on the outskirts of their village.

When they recognized him, they shouted out, "Take pity upon us, Jesus!"

As he came near to them, he could see that they were suffering from leprosy, so he said to them, "Go to the priests, so they can examine you." While they were on their way there, they were cured.

Realizing that he had become well again, one of them, a Samaritan, returned to Jesus and flung himself onto the dusty road at his feet.

"Thank you, Jesus!" he cried.

"But weren't there ten of you altogether?" asked Jesus. "What has happened to the others? Was the only one who was grateful enough to come back and thank God a foreigner?"

Jesus then looked at the man and said, "Get up and be on your way. You have been healed because you trusted in me."

CANA OF GALILEE
Israel rises from the Mediterranean coast to about 3,300 feet above sea level and then drops down to the Jordan rift valley. In general the country has warm wet winters and hot dry summers.

LEPROSY
The word Leprosy in biblical times described many skin conditions. Lepers were confined to isolated colonies to prevent the spread of the infection. They had to wear torn clothing and call out "Unclean, unclean" so that no one came near them. Today leprosy can be treated.

JESUS HEALS A LEPER
Jesus was not afraid to touch any leper who came to him for healing. His attitude contrasted sharply with other religious leaders of the time. Jesus told the man to go to the priest to be certified ritually clean so that he could become a member of society again.

The Good Samaritan

LUKE 10

Once, a teacher of the law challenged Jesus. "Teacher," he said, "tell me what I have to do to inherit eternal life."

"What does the law say?" Jesus replied.

"'Love the Lord with all your heart, soul, strength and mind' and 'Love your neighbor as much as you love yourself,'" came the answer.

"That is right," said Jesus. "If you do that, you will live."

"But who exactly is my neighbor?" the man asked. Jesus answered him with a story:

"A man was journeying from Jerusalem down the remote road that leads to the city of Jericho. He was attacked by thieves who overwhelmed him and took everything that he had, before leaving him for dead. Later, a priest came by, but all he did was cross over and continue walking as if he hadn't seen anything out of the ordinary. A Levite came along and did exactly the same. Eventually a Samaritan saw the battered body lying in the dust, was filled with compassion and immediately went to help the injured man. He bandaged him up as best he could. Then he gently eased him onto his donkey and took him to an inn.

"The next morning he had to leave, but left some money with the innkeeper saying, 'Take care of this man for me. When I return I will pay you for any extra expenses necessary for his care.'"

Jesus finished the story and then asked the teacher of the law, "Which of these three men acted as a neighbor to the man who had been so ruthlessly attacked?"

"The one who showed kindness towards him," he replied.

"Then go and do the same," Jesus concluded.

DRY WADI
This dry wadi near Jericho illustrates the barren landscape on the road from Jerusalem to Jericho, a journey of 20 miles. The quiet road descends steeply, and the rocky terrain affords many hiding places for robbers.

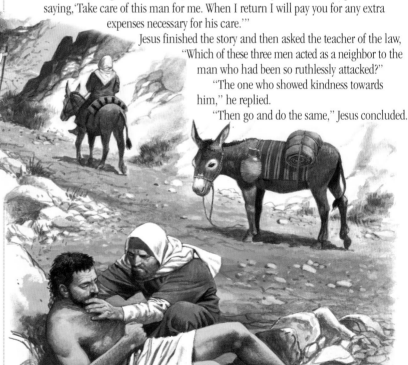

OLIVE PRESS
Olives are rich in oil which was squeezed out of them by rolling a heavy stone over them. The oil, which is recognized today as one of the healthiest sources of fat, was used for cooking and also burned in lamps. The "good Samaritan" used it as an antiseptic, but it would not have been very effective.

The great wedding feast

MATTHEW 22; LUKE 14

Jesus told the people another parable: "If you want to know what the heavenly kingdom is like, I will tell you.

"There was once a king who made extravagant preparations for the wedding feast of his son. When everything was ready he told his servants to invite the guests, but they all refused to attend.

"Undeterred, he commissioned more servants to go and fetch the guests saying, 'Inform everyone that the banquet is ready. Tell them that I have killed my finest oxen, and that the cows which have been fattened specially for the occasion are roasting on the spit. Everything is in place. All that I now lack is people to share my joy with. Come at once to my feast.'

"But the guests were not interested in going and they carried on their affairs as if nothing had happened. Some even grabbed hold of the messengers, beat them and killed them. When he heard about this, the king was livid. Consumed with anger, he called out his army and gave them orders to kill the murderers and destroy their city.

"Once more the king turned to his servants and said, 'My banquet is still waiting to be enjoyed. The guests I had hoped would come were unsuitable. So I want you to go out into the highways and byways, inviting anyone you should meet to come and share in my joy.'

"The servants set off and invited everyone they came across as they went out into the streets of the city. So many people came that the banqueting hall was full of people from every corner of society.

"Later, as the king was mingling with his guests, he came upon a man who was not dressed in the appropriate wedding clothes. 'My friend,' the king said, 'why is it that you are not wearing wedding clothes?'

"The man was at a loss for words so the king called his servants and ordered them, 'Tie this man up and expel him from my party into the night.'"

Jesus then concluded the parable by saying, "Many people are given invitations but only a few are chosen."

THE WEDDING HALL
Weddings were occasions of great rejoicing, with sumptuous foods and unlimited wine. Guests were expected to wear special clothes. To refuse an invitation was an insult. Jesus' parable shows that God invites undeserving people to participate in the blessings of his kingdom.

Jesus arrives in Jerusalem

MATTHEW 21; MARK 11; LUKE 19; JOHN 12

RIDING ON A DONKEY
In the Bible, horses were associated with war, so in peace-time kings rode donkeys instead. The donkey was a symbol of humility and peace. A donkey that had not been used before was regarded as especially suitable for religious purposes.

Jesus was on his way to Jerusalem. Before he reached the village of Bethphage by the hill called the Mount of Olives, he told two of his disciples to go ahead.

"As you enter the village, you will see a young donkey tied to the entrance of a house. Untie it and bring it here. If anyone tries to stop you, tell them that the Master needs the donkey."

So the two disciples did as Jesus had instructed. They found the donkey, and just as they were untying it, some of the villagers asked them what they were doing. "The Master needs the donkey," they replied, and with this answer they were left in peace.

Then they led the donkey back to Jesus, put some cloaks on its back as a saddle, and Jesus mounted it.

As Jesus rode into Jerusalem, his followers began to throw their cloaks onto the road in front of him. Others cut branches off palm trees and laid them down in his path.

Everyone began to sing and shout and praise God, thanking him for all the wonderful miracles they had seen Jesus perform. "Hosanna!" they shouted. "Blessed is the king who comes in God's name! Hosanna!"

Very soon, there was such a commotion that it seemed as though everyone in Jerusalem had come out to welcome Jesus.

But some Pharisees in the crowd were not impressed. They said to Jesus, "Tell your disciples not to shout in this way."

But Jesus replied, "If they were to keep quiet, the stones themselves would cry out for joy."

The signs of Christ's return

MATTHEW 24

T wo days later, as Jesus was leaving the temple, his disciples came to him and said, "Just look at these buildings!"

Jesus answered them, "Yes, they are magnificent, I know, but I tell you that not one single stone of them will be left in place; everything will be completely destroyed."

Later, when Jesus was sitting on the Mount of Olives, his disciples asked him, "Master, tell us when this will happen. What will be the sign that you are coming and that the world is coming to an end?"

"You must take great care," Jesus warned them, "because false prophets will perform miracles and claim that they are the Christ. They will lead many people away from the truth.

JESUS' LAST WEEK
Jesus rode his donkey about two miles from Bethphage across the Kidron Valley to enter Jerusalem by the Eastern Gate. The places associated with the last week of Jesus' earthly life are shown on this map.

"There will be wars and famines and earthquakes, and even the planets will shake in the sky, but try not to be afraid.

"You will see people becoming more and more wicked, and my followers will be punished and put to death," Jesus continued, as the disciples listened carefully to every word.

"Many people will turn away from me. But have courage, because I will save those who stand firm. Once the whole world has heard the truth about me, then I will be ready to return.

"I will come in the clouds for everyone to see clearly, like the lightning that flashes across the sky from east to west. And then the angels will gather my people safely together and I will take them up to heaven.

"Remember that I will come at an hour when no one expects me, so keep watch and lead good and faithful lives," Jesus encouraged them. "Make the most of all your opportunities to serve God."

This is a P³ Book
First published in 2002

P³
Queen Street House
4 Queen Street
Bath BA1 1HE, UK

Copyright © Parragon 1999

Original book produced by Miles Kelly Publishing Ltd
This edition by Design Principals, Warminster

British Library Cataloguing-in-Publication Data
A catalogue record for this book is available from the British Library

ISBN 0-75259-970-4

Printed in China